How do I feel about

BEING ANGRY

Julie Johnson

COPPER BEECH BOOKS • BROOKFIELD, CONNECTICUT

© Aladdin Books Ltd 1999
© U.S. text 1999

J
152.47
JOH

Designed and produced by
Aladdin Books Ltd
28 Percy Street
London
W1P 0LD

First published in the United States
in 1999 by
Copper Beech Books,
an imprint of
The Millbrook Press
2 Old New Milford Road
Brookfield, Connecticut 06804

Designer   Gary Edgar-Hyde
Editor   Sarah Levete
Illustrator   Christopher O'Neill
Photographer   Roger Vlitos

Printed in Belgium
5 4 3 2 1

CIP data for this publication is available
in the Library of Congress.

ISBN 0-7613-0910-1 (lib. bdg.)

Contents

Introduction

Connor, Jason, Leah, Marsha, and Sim live on the same street. They are good friends. They all know what it is like to feel angry or what it is like when others get angry with them. Join them as they share their feelings about being angry and how they deal with it.

I get angry when I can't do my school work.

I get angry with friends and then we fall out.

It's important to deal with anger without upsetting other people.

SIM

MARSHA

CONNOR

LEAH

People get angry for lots of different reasons.

It helps to talk to people about your feelings.

JASON

What is Anger?

After school, Connor is telling Leah he's been angry all day because his little brother took his favorite game without asking. Connor felt so angry he shouted at his brother and made him cry. Anger is a feeling that can last a short time or a long time. It can make you behave in different ways.

What's the matter?

My brother made me really angry.

You may break something in anger.

4

You may shout in anger.

▼ Anger Is A Feeling

Anger is a feeling, like fear or sadness. If you are having a good day and something happens to make you angry, the anger may disappear quickly.

If lots of things have upset you the anger may last for a long time. It can rumble away inside you, waiting to burst out.

◀ It Can Be Sudden

People get angry about all sorts of things and for lots of different reasons. Their anger may burst out suddenly, without any warning. Anger can make people say or do mean things.

Leah, what does being angry mean to you?

"Being angry is when you are so mad you say mean things. It can make you want to break something or hurt someone.

"Being angry can make you want to cry because you don't know what else to do."

5

Being Angry With People

Marsha and Leah are best friends, but they have had an argument.

They are so angry that they aren't speaking to each other.

Can you remember when you last got angry with someone?

Who were you angry with?

Can you remember what you were angry about?

You may get angry at school or…

6

… you may get angry at home.

Being Angry With People

1. Simon was waiting for Paulo to arrive.

2. Simon rang to find out where Paulo was.

3. Paulo had arranged to do something else. Simon threw down his toy.

Why was Simon angry?

Paulo let Simon down. He didn't even say he was sorry. Simon's feelings were hurt.

Instead of breaking his toy, it would have been better if Simon had told Paulo how he felt. Then Paulo may have realized how thoughtless he had been. Simon could have talked to his dad about how upset he felt.

▼ Best Friends

Even your best friends can make you angry. It may be something they do or say. You may see things differently from one another.

You may say, or even do, something unkind. That will only make the situation worse. It won't make you feel better.

Oh, I took that book to school.

◄ Brothers And Sisters

If you have a brother or sister, do you get angry with him or her? Perhaps he or she borrowed something without asking? Try to explain how you feel — although your brother or sister may not listen to you. If you feel very angry, talk to your parents.

You can't go to Sam's today.

▶ Why Not?

There will be times when a teacher or parent won't allow you to do something. Sulking, shouting, or crashing around won't change their mind. Try to explain why you feel angry. Give them time to explain their reasons.

8

Being Angry With People

▼ It's All Her Fault!

When someone has let you down, it can make you feel very angry. You may want to shout at the person you are mad at. But being angry won't change the situation. Try to remember that the person may be feeling bad anyway.

You stupid *!***!!

Sorry!

◄ It Was A Mistake!

Some people get angry easily, when there isn't much to be angry about. Without thinking, they may hit out with words, or even physically, at someone who they think has wronged them. If you do this, it is important to say you're sorry.

Marsha is angry because...

"I told Leah a secret and she told someone else. That wasn't fair."

Leah is angry because...

"I didn't think Marsha would mind. Then I got angry because Marsha said some really mean things to me."

Being Angry With Yourself

In the playground, Jason is talking to Sim who was sent out of class for losing his temper and hitting another pupil. Sim got angry because he he was having difficulty reading a book. Have you ever gotten angry with yourself? Did you take your angry feelings out on yourself or out on someone else?

1. Sabrina was building a matchstick model of a house for her school project.

2. She was finding one piece really hard to fix in place.

3. Sabrina became so angry that she knocked the model over and spoiled it.

Why was Sabrina angry?

Sabrina had been enjoying building the house. When she came to a tricky part she lost her patience because she couldn't do it. She became frustrated and angry.

By getting angry with herself, rather than asking for some help, she stopped enjoying what she was doing. She ruined what she had been doing well up to that point.

Being Angry With Yourself

▷ *Why Did I Say That?*

Sometimes people say hurtful things without thinking. They don't always realize that what they are saying is hurtful or unkind. When they think about it later, they may feel angry with themselves for having been thoughtless.

Oh, why did I say that to him? I'm so stupid.

⚠ *I Can't Do It!*

You may get mad if you are trying to learn a new skill and find it quite difficult! You may get impatient and frustrated and want to give up.

Try to remember that it takes a while to get the hang of new things. Practice makes perfect!

Sim, why did you hit out?

"I got so angry because I couldn't read. Being angry with myself made me angry with everyone else. I didn't think and I just hit another boy. It was really unfair because he hadn't done anything to upset me.

"I can't always stop feeling angry, but I can stop doing or saying hurtful things."

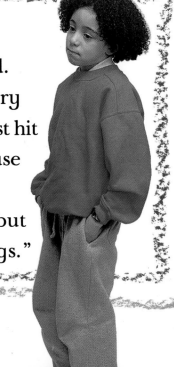

12

Being Angry Makes You Feel...

This morning, Connor got so angry he hit his brother, Ben.
He realizes he shouldn't have done this. He has hurt his
brother, and his mom is now angry with him.
It's important not to hit out at people, however angry you
feel. It will make the situation worse — and it won't make you
feel any better.

Anger can make you feel out of control.

13

Anger can make you upset.

▼ *Angry and Lonely*

Some people seem to be angry all the time. They take their anger out on friends. It may be that they haven't learned to control their anger.

Friends may put up with this for a while, but may soon choose other friends.

◀ *Angry and Upset*

Anger can lead to lots of other feelings. You may feel frightened by your anger or it can make you feel lonely. You may feel miserable and upset because you don't understand or know what to do with your angry feelings.

Don't let Daniel play because he gets mad at you if you miss a shot.

Connor, how do you feel now?

"I was wrong to hit my brother, but I wasn't wrong to feel angry. I should have told my mom how angry I felt instead of hitting Ben.

"Everyone feels angry sometimes, but it's what you do with your anger that can make the problems."

Hiding Other Feelings

Sim has told his teacher that he got angry because he was embarrassed and frustrated that he couldn't read. His teacher explained that some of us just take longer than others to learn to do something. Jason feels more settled in his new home now but at first he felt angry because he was unhappy with all the changes. Sometimes anger can hide different feelings.

Anger can hide a feeling of embarrassment.

15

It can hide a difficulty with learning.

1. Adam was being bullied by a gang.

2. It made him angry toward his family and toward his good friends.

3. Adam's best friend decided to tell Adam's mom what was going on.

Why was Adam feeling angry?

Adam was being bullied. He was frightened, confused, and upset. Getting angry with the people he loved covered up these feelings.

It would have been better if Adam had told his parents or a teacher about the bullying. They would have been able to help.

▽ *That Doesn't Feel* OK

If someone touches you and it doesn't feel right, or if they try to make you do something you know is wrong, you may feel angry. You may feel angry if someone asks you to keep a secret that you are not happy about. If this happens, it is important to talk to a grown-up who you trust.

◁ *Problems At Home*

You may feel left out if a new baby arrives or you may feel confused if your parents are separating or divorcing. These feelings can make you angry. It can help to talk to a grown-up, although it may not make the situation change.

Jason, do you get angry easily?

"I only recently came to this part of the country with my family. It meant lots of changes. People teased me at school because of my accent. That made me angry.

"I was scared at all the new things that were happening. That made me angry, too."

17

If Someone Is Angry With You

Leah's mom gets angry with her when Leah doesn't tidy her room. Sim says his dad never used to lose his temper, but since he lost his job and is stuck at home all day, he always seems angry.

Can you remember who was last angry with you and why?

Mom gets angry because she says my room is messy.

My dad is always in a bad mood and angry.

You may not know why someone is angry...

... or you may know very well.

▼ *Saying Sorry*

If a friend is angry with you because you have let him or her down, why not say you're sorry?

If you don't understand why a friend is angry with you, try to talk about it. It helps to ask a grown-up to help you both talk together.

◀ *Angry Grown-ups*

Grown-ups may get mad at you because you have been naughty or have disobeyed them. Perhaps they have had a bad day at work, are not happy, or maybe someone is angry with them. Grown-ups may take their anger out on someone else, just like you can.

Leah, what do you do when your mom is angry with you?

"If it's because I've been naughty, I say I'm sorry and try not to do it again. If mom gets angry because she's tired or worried, I try not to get upset by it. If I feel fed up about it, I talk to my grandma."

Dealing with Angry Feelings

Marsha talked to her mom about why she was angry with Leah. Leah drew a picture of how angry and upset she felt. The next time they saw each other they were able to talk about why they were angry. Now, they have made up.

Try writing down how you feel.

Try counting to ten.

▽ *Put It On Paper*

Try to remember that it's when you let anger get out of control that the problems start. You can't stop feeling angry, but you can take time to think about why you may be feeling angry.

Try to write down how you feel — or paint an angry picture!

◁ *Ask For Help*

If you have had a very bad argument with a friend that you can't sort out, why not ask your parents to help?

If you are worried about how angry you feel, talk to a grown-up you trust. Ask him or her what they do when they get angry.

These are Marsha and Leah's tips for ways to deal with anger.

"Think before you do or say anything. Think about what is making you angry. Explain calmly how you feel. Punch a pillow or take a deep breath. Try not to take your anger out on others. If you do, be prepared to say you're sorry."

Don't Forget...

Sim, how is your reading?

"Now that I don't get so angry it's a bit easier. It's still hard not to blow up, but I try to count to ten before I try a difficult word again. You can't stop angry feelings, but you can stop yourself from being unkind or hurtful to other people. It's important to talk to someone about what is making you angry."

Leah, what do you do when your mom is angry?

"Sometimes it makes me angry that she is angry with me, when I haven't even done anything wrong! Then I tell my grandma how I feel and that helps me to understand that my mom still loves me — even when she's mad."

Marsha, how do you cope with anger?

"Anger is a very strong feeling. It can come on you very quickly. But you can learn to use it and be in control of it. It's not always easy and it takes time to learn."

Connor, do you still get angry with your brother?

"I'm going to work out how to share some of my things with my younger brother but I'm going to make sure he can't reach things that I really don't want him to borrow."

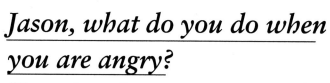

Jason, what do you do when you are angry?

"Sometimes I go to my room and shout very loudly or punch a soft pillow. That makes me feel better!"

23

Index

All the photographs in this book have been posed by models. The publishers would like to thank them all.